The do-it-yourself Guide to...

Planning the (nearly) Perfect Wedding

by
Marianne Richmond

Do:
call the ~~b~~...
schedule
the florist
— book the band

dress fitting
2:30 Friday!

The do-it-yourself Guide to...
Planning the (nearly) Perfect Wedding

Marianne Richmond Studios, Inc.
420 N. 5th Street, Suite 840
Minneapolis, MN 55401
www.mariannerichmond.com

ISBN 0-9774651-8-7

Illustrations by Marianne Richmond

Book design by Sara Dare Biscan

Printed in China

First Printing

TO

FROM

Date

Congratulations, you're getting married!
   And you want your day to be
absolutely perfect.

While "perfect" is an understandable goal —
   it is just not reality, girlfriend.
You're talking about orchestrating one of
   the most joyful days of your life
which involves you, a million decisions,
   and... other people! Other people

with moods, agendas, flaws and minds of their own.

Well, bride-to-be — cheer up! We have created just for you The do-it-yourself Guide to Planning the (nearly) Perfect Wedding... the helpful little resource for figuring out what's really worth the time, effort and emotion to create a wonderfully memorable day!

Brush up on your people skills.

During the wedding planning process, you'll need to navigate the emotional needs of your key players — your mother, his mother, your bridesmaids, the florist, the photographer, the caterer, the organist …

Keep these affirming phrases at the ready:

I hear what you're saying.

Can I share with you how you are a special part of

a wonderful plan?

That's an interesting point you bring up.

What would make you feel more valued and loved?

I'll take it under advisement.

And when you simply must pull rank?

It's **MY** wedding and if I don't get my way, I'll cry!

Be nice to your bridesmaids.

These women are supposedly some of your favorite people. They WILL potentially band together and sabotage your day for unreasonable financial demands, green chiffon gowns that make their butts look like Mack trucks, and the requirement that they must participate in the Dollar Dance at the reception.

And get real about the bridesmaid dress thing.

You'll tell them they can wear their dress again.

Forget it — once a bridesmaid dress, always a bridesmaid dress.

**Don't obsess about
the small stuff.**

Will it <u>really</u> matter that the
ribbons for the favors are baby
blue instead of Mediterranean
Ocean-at-sunset blue?

Befriend a budget!

We know, we know. The word, "budget," gets a bad rap, inspiring feelings of lack, deprivation, and less-than. That a magazine exists called **Tightwight Gazette** does not help.

So, make budget <u>sexy</u>. Call yourself the "Budget Babe" and dream about

all the things you'll be able to buy
down the road if you save money now —
a house, vacations and new furniture!

Better to spend wisely on one wedding day

than to have first-years-of marriage full of lack,

deprivation and less-than!

Mr. and Mrs. John Smith
request the honour of your presence
at the marriage of their daughter
Jennifer Marie Smith
to
Mr. Timothy Andrew Jones
son of Mr. and Mrs. Andrew Jones

Saturday, the twentieth of May
Two thousand and six
6:00 pm
St. Paul's Church
Reception to immediately follow

In lieu of gifts, the couple requests cash
to fuel their lifestyle

Wedding invitation etiquette:

It's really <u>not</u> okay to ask for money toward your new boat, your IRA or your future timeshare.

Repeat after us:
"I cannot control the weather."

That's right — you cannot control the weather on your wedding day.

Gluing yourself to the Weather Channel 24/7, tracking high

and low pressure fronts, and learning about cirrus, stratus,

and cumulus clouds will not change this fact.

Have a plan B for outdoor wedding plans.

Emblazon this thought in your mind:

People who attend your wedding care about the drinks, the music and the food. And quite likely in that order.

Not the centerpieces, the personalized fortune cookies or the bouquet toss.

Music sets the mood.

Cool, fun band or DJ makes
cool, fun wedding.

Cheesy DJ makes bad memories of

Grandma doing the Chicken Dance.

A photographer has

ultimate power.

Choose yours wisely.
Now is _not_ the time to
give the neighbor boy his
chance to complete his
photography class project.

Ask questions.

See samples.

Read the fine print.

And be sure he knows your best angles.

p.s. Same advice for the videographer!

Maintain the 'you' that people
know and love.

You want to look memorable, but
    don't forget to be recognizable.

Too much hairdo, makeup, and diet
    is often... too much.

You don't want Grandpa Charlie wondering who
the bride is when he thought he was coming to
your wedding.

Maybe temper the tanning booth, too.

Orangey-brown doesn't go with wedding white.

Ixnay on the oozing-bay.

Getting drunk the night before
your wedding is not a good idea.
The last thing you need when
wanting to be the star of your day
is to wake up with a headache, puffy
skin, fuzzy head, and stomach ache.

Getting drunk at your reception is not a very good

idea either. Not remembering your wedding day

would qualify later on as a huge regret.

Don't spaz at the glass clinkers.

We know you're dying to swallow a morsel of food, but people love this part where they clink and you kiss.

May as well indulge them.

If you ever hear yourself thinking,
"this would be kinda corny
but we should ..."

STOP. Don't do it.

It, whatever it is, WILL be corny – and the thing

people talk about for years.

Practice restraint.

As much as you could blame
pre-wedding jitters — you
must realize your wedding
"eve" is not the time to take
issue with how he chews his
food, his hairstyle, or his
unnaturally close relationship
with his mother.

Ditto on the restraint thing.

A couple things <u>not</u> to say on your
wedding night while you're,
um, "celebrating":

Did you know the ceiling
needs painting?

Did I remember to take my pill?

Honey, I have a confession to make...

Aim for a nearly perfect day.

Since the day Adam ate that darn apple, nothing
about the world has been perfect – so why put
all that pressure on yourself?

And remember —
you can always elope!

Your family will eventually
get over it....

A gifted author and artist, Marianne Richmond shares
her creations with millions of people worldwide
through her delightful books, cards, and giftware.
In addition to the *simply said...* and *smartly said...*
gift book series, she has written and illustrated eight
additional books: **The Gift of an Angel,
The Gift of a Memory, Hooray for You!,
The Gifts of Being Grand, I Love You So....,
My Shoes Take Me Where I Want to Go,
Dear Daughter,** and **Dear Son**

To learn more about Marianne's products, please visit
www.mariannerichmond.com.